Basic Supplies

- black & white alphabet tiles from *Paper Pizazz® Alphabet Tiles #2*
- scissors
- acid-free adhesive: Glue Dots™ or stick glue
- tracing paper
- transfer paper
- black fine tip permanent pen
- decorating chalks by Craf-T Products

Tearing Paper

When tearing the papers for the borders of each spread, use the color photo as a guide. Tear the 5½"x8½" piece of paper in half then tear more off of each piece for your desired width.

Paper Pizazz® papers are printed on a white background. When you tear the paper in an upward motion the piece that you have torn away will not have a white tear line. The other piece will have a white torn edge.

For controlled tearing: Place the paper on the edge of a table while tearing or use a liner paintbrush to apply a thin line of water where you want to make the tear. Tear the paper while it is still damp and it will only tear along this line. Allow the paper to dry and then continue.

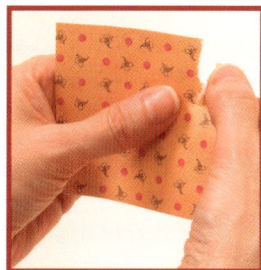

Setting Eyelets

Tools: Anywhere hole punch, eyelet setter, hammer and mat.

1 From the front of the paper, use the anywhere punch or a handheld punch to make a hole, then insert the eyelet.

2 Turn the paper and eyelet over. From the back of the paper, use the hammer and eyelet setter to pound down the edge of the eyelet to secure it.

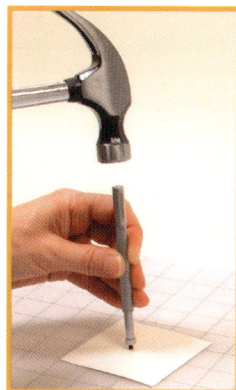

Basic I

1 Mat t[...] each o[...] background mat with a border between ⅛ –¼ wide. All of the papers used are available by the sheet or in books (the book titles are listed in italics).

2 **Trace & transfer the patterns:** Trace the pattern from this book. Lay the tracing paper over your paper with transfer paper between them. Retrace the pattern, then cut out your paper. Transferring the pattern to the back of the paper can eliminate the need to erase pencil marks. The gray lines and circles indicate where to add the penwork. Cut out with a sharp pair of straight-edge scissors.

3 **Add the penwork:** Drawing a wavy line border around the tan squares is much easier than trying to draw perfectly straight lines—they also add a touch of whimsy. Use pens to add detail to the paper pieced images, such as eyes, shown in gray or white on each pattern.

4 **Chalk the pieces:** One way to add depth and highlights to your pieces is to use decorating chalks. Use a cosmetic applicator, cotton swab or your fingertip to apply chalk around the edge of the alphabet tiles and paper pieces. For example, the black chalk on the key adds dimension. We've listed the chalk colors in the You Will Need lists.

decorating chalks from Craf-T Products

5 **Assemble the pieces:** Refer to the color photo to arrange the pieces as shown. Some pieces will be on top of others, so be sure you like the placement before gluing them together.

1

A is for Apple,

high up in a tree

You will need:
patterned Paper Pizazz®: stars on yellow (available by the sheet)
solid Paper Pizazz®:
- *navy blue, red, green, dark green (Teresa's Handpicked Solid Jewel Tones)*
- *orange, light tan, brown, gray, blue (Teresa's Handpicked Solid Muted Colors)*
- *goldenrod (Plain Brights)*
- *white (New Plain Pastels)*
decorating chalks: red, light blue, black, white
6" length of jute twine
1/16" hole punch
optional: 1/4" star punch
basic supplies (see page 1)

1 Cut two 5½"x8½" stars on yellow rectangles. Cut a 5½"x8½" piece of navy blue paper and tear it into two borders (see page 1). Glue one piece of navy paper to a stars piece with the tears facing the inside of the spread.

2 Mat your photo on white. Mat it again on red with a torn border. Glue it centered on the left hand page.

3 Cut out two "A" alphabet tiles and chalk the checkerboards with red. Mat each tile onto a 1¼" white square and outline them with a black wavy double border as shown. Glue one to each page. Hand write or computer print your words on white paper. Use the pen to add a black border then chalk the "A" word red. Glue them to the left hand page.

4 Cut three 2¼" tan squares. Use the black pen to outline each square with a wavy double border as shown. Mat one on green, one on goldenrod and one on red, each with a ¼" border.

5 Use the patterns to cut out the apple, clouds, airplane and anchor. Glue each to a tan square as shown then glue them to the right hand page.

is for Apple,

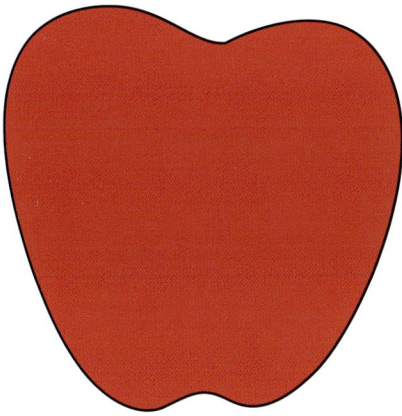

Apple: Cut one from red paper then shade the edge with black chalk. Highlight the top left with white chalk.

Leaf: Cut two from dark green paper then shade the edge with black chalk.

Stem: Cut one from brown paper then shade the edge with black chalk.

Cloud: Cut two from white paper then shade the edge with light blue chalk.

Nose: Cut one from orange paper then shade the edge with black chalk.

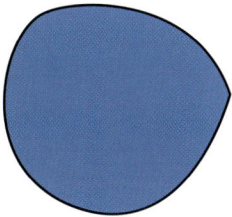

Wing: Cut one from blue paper then shade the edge with black chalk.

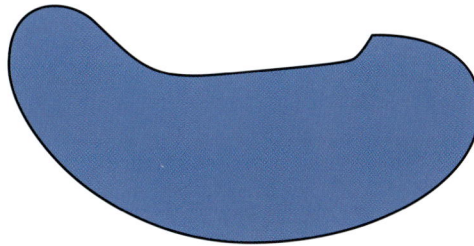

Body: Cut one from blue paper then shade the edge with black chalk.

Tail: Cut one from blue paper then shade the edge with black chalk.

Propeller: Cut one from gray paper then shade the edge with black chalk.

high up in a tree

Star: Cut one from red paper, or use the star punch.

Twine: Knot one end then thread the twine through the hole. Wrap the loose end around the anchor as shown in the photo on page 2.

Anchor: Cut one from gray paper then shade the edge with black chalk. Punch out the hole.

B is for Bike ride,

with my family

1 Cut two 5½"x8½" light blue rectangles. Cut a 5½"x8½" piece of green dots paper and tear it into two borders (see page 1). Glue one piece of dot paper to a blue piece with the tears facing the inside of the spread.

2 Mat your photo on white. Mat it again on black with a torn border. Glue it centered on the left hand page.

3 Cut out two "B" alphabet tiles and chalk the checkerboards with light blue. Mat each tile onto a 1¼" white square and outline them with a black wavy double border as shown. Glue one to each page. Hand write or computer print your words on white paper. Use the pen to add a black border then chalk the "B" word light blue. Glue them to the left hand page.

4 Cut three 2¼" tan squares. Use the black pen to outline each square with a wavy double border as shown. Mat one on navy blue, one on goldenrod and one on red, each with a ¼" border.

5 Use the patterns to cut out the baseball, the paper for the buttons and the books. Glue each to a tan square as shown then glue them to the right hand page.

Health

Science

Reading

B

is for Bike ride,

Baseball: Cut one from speckled paper then use the black pen to outline it. Shade the edge and where the X's will go with brown chalk. Stitch the X's with red embroidery thread.

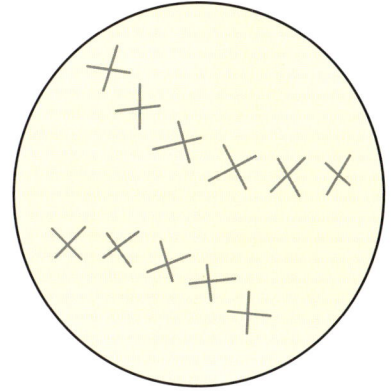

Button mat: Cut one from speckled paper then tear each side. Chalk the edges with brown then glue on the buttons.

with my family

Health Book: Cut one from red paper then shade the edge with black chalk.

Health

Science Book: Cut one from mustard yellow cardstock then shade the edge with black chalk.

Science

Reading Book: Cut one from dark burgundy paper then shade the edge with black chalk.

Reading

Science Book: Cut one from brown paper then draw the stitches with the white pen.

Reading Book: Cut one from black paper.

5

is for Crying,

as sad as sad can be

C

You will need:

*patterned Paper Pizazz®: yellow swirls on blue
  (available by the sheet)*
solid Paper Pizazz®:
  • *navy blue, red, green (Teresa's Handpicked
    Solid Jewel Tones)*
  • *gray, light tan, dark purple, black, light
    brown, light yellow, speckled (Teresa's
    Handpicked Solid Muted Colors)*
  • *goldenrod (Plain Brights)*
  • *white (New Plain Pastels)*
decorating chalks: red, brown, black, light blue
white liquid appliqué or white dimensional paint
⅛" nickel brad
½" bear punch
aluminum foil
basic supplies (see page 1)

1 Cut two 5½"x8½" yellow swirls rectangles. Cut a
5½"x8½" piece of light yellow paper and tear it into two
borders (see page 1). Glue one piece of yellow paper to a
swirls piece with the tears facing the inside of the spread.

2 Mat your photo on white. Mat it again on red with a torn
border. Glue it centered on the left hand page.

3 Cut out two "C" alphabet tiles and chalk the
checkerboards with red. Mat each tile onto a 1¼" white
square and outline them with a black wavy double border as
shown. Glue one to each page. Hand write or computer print
your words on white paper. Use the pen to add a black border
then chalk the "C" word red. Glue them to the left hand page.

4 Cut three 2¼" tan squares. Use the black pen to outline
each square with a wavy double border as shown. Mat
one on red, one on navy blue and one on green, each with a
¼" border.

5 Use the patterns to cut out the cookie sheet, clock and
car. Punch out three bears. Glue each to a tan square as
shown then glue them to the right hand page.

is for Crying,

Cookie sheet: Cut one from white paper and cover with aluminum foil. Glue the edges to the back.

Cookies: Punch three bears from light brown paper. "Ice" them with liquid appliqué or paint with dimensional paint and let dry overnight.

Clock frame: Cut one from dark purple paper.

Clock face: Cut one from speckled paper. Draw the numbers with the black pen. Shade the edge with brown chalk.

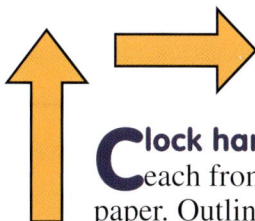

Clock hands: Cut one each from goldenrod paper. Outline them with the black pen. Attach them to the clock face with the brad.

as sad as sad can be

Windows: Cut one each from white paper and shade the edges with light blue chalk.

Car: Cut one from red paper and shade the edge with black chalk.

Tail pipe: Cut one from red paper.

Headlight: Cut one from goldenrod paper.

Exhaust: Cut one from gray paper and shade the edge with black chalk.

Wheels: Cut two from black paper.

Door handle: Cut one from goldenrod paper.

7

D is for Dog...

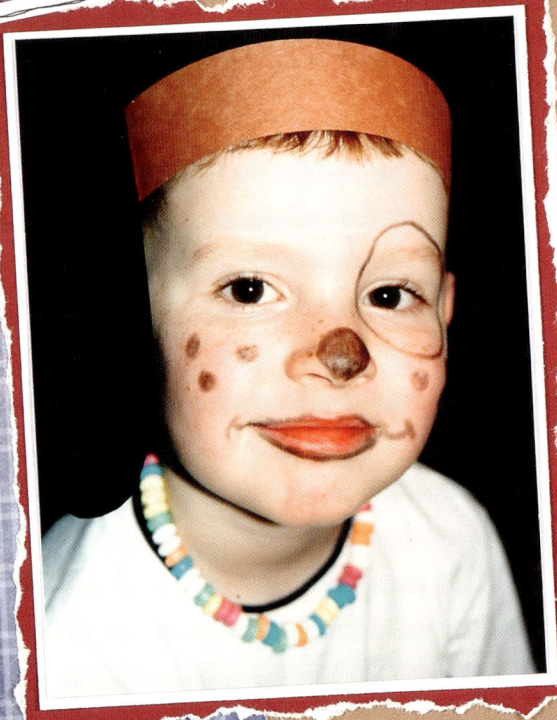

or is that really Westley?

You will need:

patterned Paper Pizazz®:
blue plaid (Coordinating
Florals & Patterns, also
available by the sheet)
specialty Paper Pizazz®:
white vellum (Vellum
Papers)
solid Paper Pizazz®:
• *navy blue, red, green,*
(Teresa's Handpicked
Solid Jewel Tones)
• *light brown, light tan,*
(Teresa's Handpicked
Solid Muted Colors)

• *goldenrod (Plain*
Brights)
• *white (New Plain*
Pastels)
decorating chalks: red,
green, black
2"x4" piece of ivory felt
⅛" brads: nickel, brown
1" long silver safety pin
24-gauge silver craft wire
needle nose pliers
basic supplies (see page 1)

1 Cut two 5½"x8½" light brown rectangles. Cut a 5½"x8½" piece of blue plaid paper and tear it into two borders (see page 1). Glue one piece of plaid paper to a brown piece with the tears facing the inside of the spread.

2 Mat your photo on white. Mat it again on red with a torn border. Glue it centered on the left hand page.

3 Cut out two "D" alphabet tiles and chalk the checkerboards with red. Mat each tile onto a 1¼" white square and outline them with a black wavy double border as shown. Glue one to each page. Hand write or computer print your words on white paper. Use the pen to add a black border then chalk the "D" word red. Glue them to the left hand page.

4 Cut three 2¼" tan squares. Use the black pen to outline each square with a wavy double border as shown. Mat one on green, one on goldenrod and one on navy blue, each with a ¼" border.

5 Use the patterns to cut out the diaper, door and dragonfly. Glue each to a tan square as shown then glue them to the right hand page.

8

is for Dog...

Diaper: Cut one from felt and fold on the dashed line. Use the safety pin to hold it closed at the top.

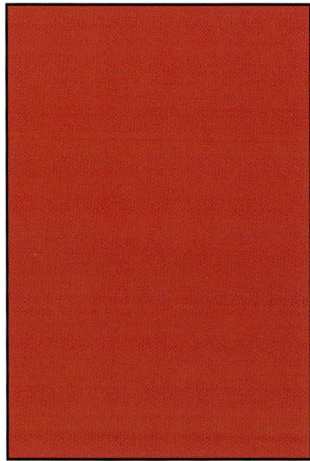

Door: Cut one from red then shade the edges with black chalk.

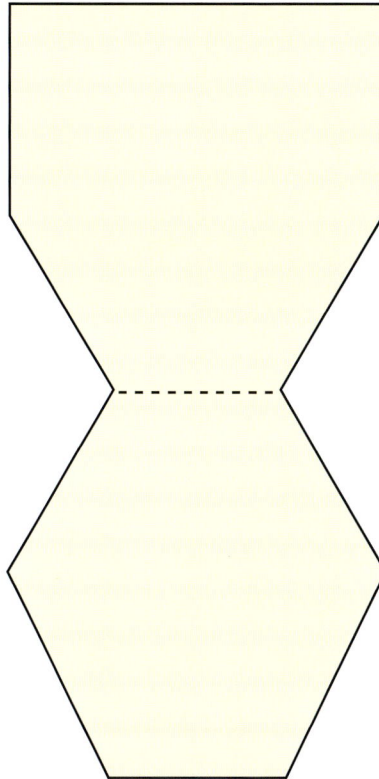

Door panels: Cut six from white.

Door frame: Cut one from white then use the black pen to add the penwork.

Door panels: Cut six from red then shade each corner with black chalk. Glue one to each white square.

Dragonfly body: Cut one from navy blue then shade the edge with black chalk.

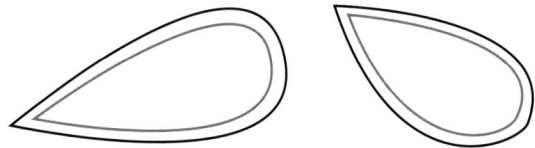

Wings: Cut one of each from white vellum then outline each with the black pen. Let the ink dry then shade the center of each wing with green chalk.

Antennae: Use the patterns and pliers to shape one of each from silver wire.

or is that really *"child's name"* ?

9

E is for Eating, a big plate of food

You will need:

patterned Paper Pizazz®:
- *yellow swirls (Bright Tints, also available by the sheet)*

solid Paper Pizazz®:
- *navy blue, red, green, dark green (Teresa's Handpicked Solid Jewel Tones)*
- *gray, light tan, light purple, brown (Teresa's Handpicked Solid Muted Colors)*

- *goldenrod (Plain Brights)*
- *white, light aqua (New Plain Pastels)*

decorating chalks: pink, light blue, purple, black
mustard yellow cardstock
three 12" lengths of raffia
3" length of red embroidery floss
hole punches: 1/8", 1/4"
basic supplies (see page 1)

1 Cut two 5½"x8½" yellow swirls rectangles. Cut a 5½"x8½" piece of navy blue paper and tear it into two borders (see page 1). Glue one piece of navy paper to a swirls piece with the tears facing the inside of the spread.

2 Mat your photo on white. Mat it again on red with a torn border. Glue it centered on the left hand page.

3 Cut out two "E" alphabet tiles and chalk the checkerboards with light blue. Mat each tile onto a 1¼" white square and outline them with a black wavy double border as shown. Glue one to each page. Hand write or computer print your words on white paper. Use the pen to add a black border then chalk the "E" word light blue. Glue them to the left hand page.

4 Cut three 2¼" tan squares. Use the black pen to outline each square with a wavy double border as shown. Mat one on red, one on goldenrod and one on green, each with a ¼" border.

5 Use the patterns to cut out the elephant, grass, egg, label and envelope. Glue each to a tan square as shown then glue them to the right hand page.

First Class

E

Body: Cut one from gray and shade the edge with black chalk.

Ears: Cut one of each from gray and shade the edges with black chalk. Shade the inner ears with pink chalk.

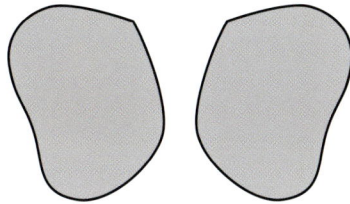

Head: Cut one from gray and shade the edge with black chalk. Use the black pen to draw the eyes. Blush the cheek with pink chalk.

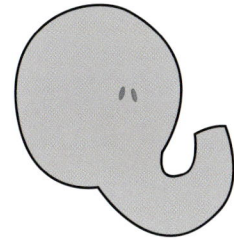

Grass: Cut one from dark green paper.

is for Eating,

Swirl dots: Punch seven ¼" circles from light aqua. Use the black pen to draw the swirl on each. Glue them to the egg.

Egg: Cut one from light purple and shade the edge with purple chalk.

Raffia: Wrap three strands around the egg and tie a bow in the front.

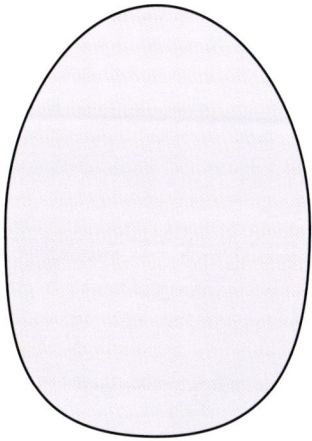

a big plate of food

Label: Cut one from white paper and add black penwork.

First Class

Envelope: Cut one from mustard yellow cardstock. Fold in the side flaps on the dashed lines and glue them together. Fold up the bottom flap and glue it to the side flaps. Fold down the top flap.

Circle: Cut one from brown paper. Glue it to the center of the top flap. Punch a ⅛" hole in the center of the brown circle and the flap.

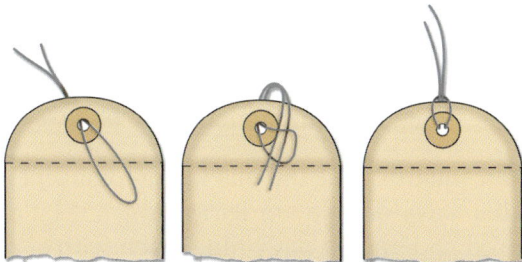

Embroidery floss: Fold the floss in half and thread the fold through the hole from the inside of the flap. Thread the loose ends through the folded end then pull to remove the slack.

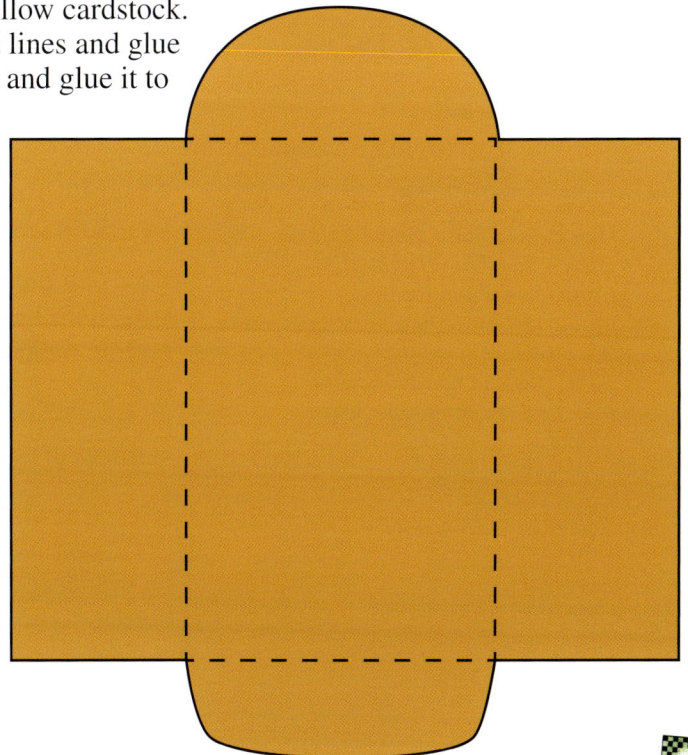

11

F is for Fish I caught,

when the fishing was good

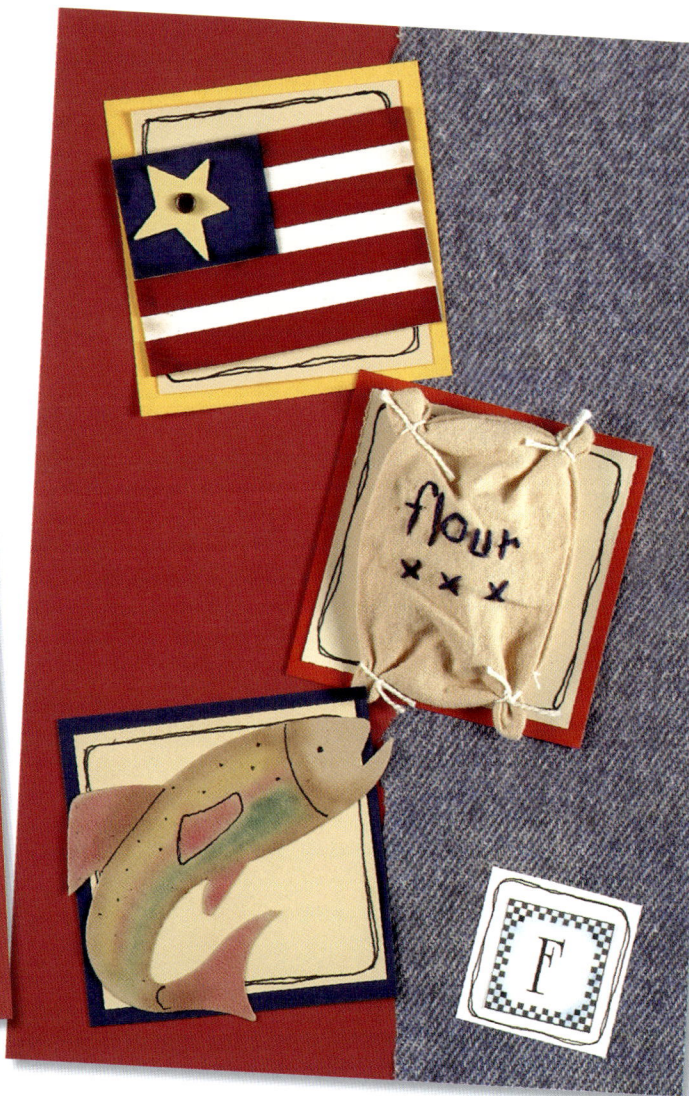

You will need:

patterned Paper Pizazz®: denim (available by the sheet)
solid Paper Pizazz®:
- *navy blue, red (Teresa's Handpicked Solid Jewel Tones)*
- *yellow, light tan, light brown (Teresa's Handpicked Solid Muted Colors)*
- *goldenrod (Plain Brights)*
- *white (New Plain Pastels)*

decorating chalks: light blue, yellow, green, pink, brown, black
2¼"x5½" piece of natural muslin
embroidery floss: navy blue, white
tan thread
sewing needle
⅛" brown brad
basic supplies (see page 1)

1 Cut two 5½"x8½" red rectangles. Cut a 5½"x8½" piece of denim paper and tear it into two borders (see page 1). Glue one piece of denim paper to a red piece with the tears facing the inside of the spread.

2 Mat your photo on white. Mat it again on goldenrod with a torn border. Glue it centered on the left hand page.

3 Cut out two "F" alphabet tiles and chalk the checkerboards with light blue. Mat each tile onto a 1¼" white square and outline them with a black wavy double border as shown. Glue one to each page. Hand write or computer print your words on white paper. Use the pen to add a black border then chalk the word that starts with "F" light blue. Glue them to the left hand page.

4 Cut three 2¼" tan squares. Use the black pen to outline each square with a wavy double border as shown. Mat one on goldenrod, one on red and one on navy blue, each with a ¼" border.

5 Use the patterns to cut out the flag, flour sack and fish. Glue each to a tan square as shown then glue them to the right hand page.

Flag: Cut one from white paper and shade the edges with brown chalk.

is for Fish I caught,

Star: Cut one from yellow paper. Attach it to the blue rectangle with the brad.

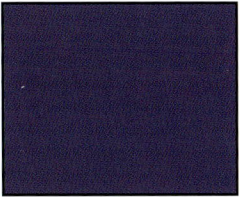

Flag: Cut one from navy blue paper and shade the edges with black chalk.

Flag stripes: Cut four from red paper and shade the ends of each strip with brown chalk.

Flour sack: Cut one from muslin. Stitch "flour" and the X's with navy blue embroidery floss. Fold the muslin in half with the stitching on the inside then use tan thread to sew three sides together. Turn right-side out and sew the opening closed. Tie each corner with white floss, trimming the ends to ¼".

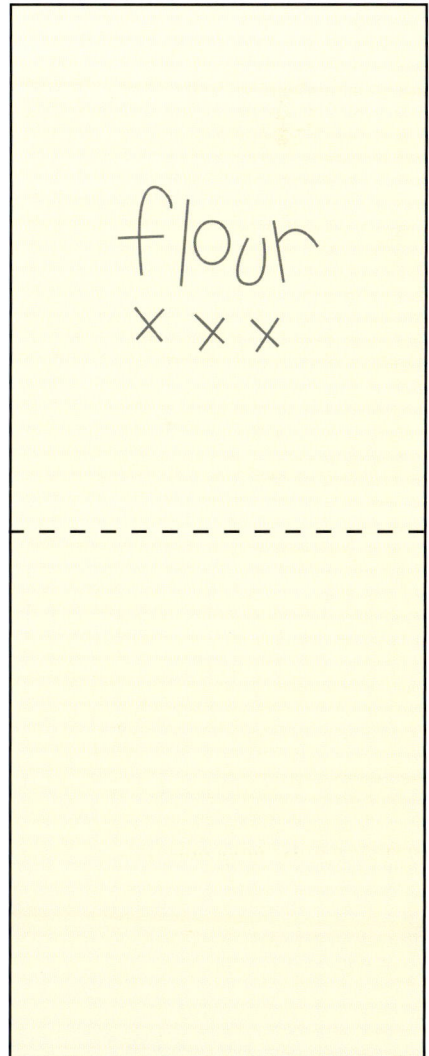

flour
x x x

when the fishing was good

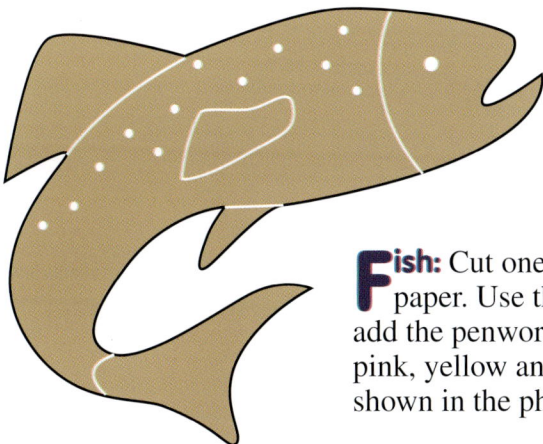

Fish: Cut one from light brown paper. Use the black pen to add the penwork. Chalk with pink, yellow and light blue as shown in the photo on page 12.

G is for Grandma,

who brings us so much joy

You will need:
patterned Paper Pizazz®: yellow stripes (Soft Tints, also available by the sheet)
solid Paper Pizazz®:
- navy blue, red, green (Teresa's Handpicked Solid Jewel Tones)
- light tan, brown (Teresa's Handpicked Solid Muted Colors)
- goldenrod (Plain Brights)
- white, ivory (New Plain Pastels)
mustard yellow cardstock
1"x3" rectangle of cardstock (any color)
decorating chalks: pink, light blue, brown
1½"x3½" rectangle of aluminum foil
4" length of dark yellow embroidery floss
basic supplies (see page 1)

1 Cut two 5½"x8½" yellow stripe rectangles. Cut a 5½"x8½" piece of red paper and tear it into two borders (see page 1). Glue one piece of red to a stripe piece with the tears facing the inside of the spread.

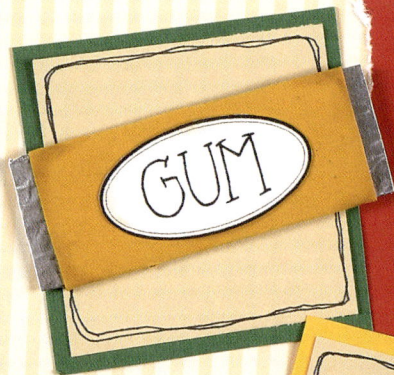

2 Mat your photo on white. Mat it again on navy blue with a torn border. Glue it centered on the left hand page.

3 Cut out two "G" alphabet tiles and chalk the checkerboards with light blue. Mat each tile onto a 1¼" white square and outline them with a black wavy double border as shown. Glue one to each page. Hand write or computer print your words on white paper. Use the pen to add a black border then chalk the "G" word light blue. Glue them to the left hand page.

4 Cut three 2¼" tan squares. Use the black pen to outline each square with a wavy double border as shown. Mat one on green, one on goldenrod and one on navy blue, each with a ¼" border.

5 Use the patterns to cut out the gum, girl and ghost. Glue each to a tan square as shown then glue them to the right hand page.

GUM

GUM

Gum wrapper: Cut one from cardstock. Wrap the rectangle with aluminum foil, gluing the sides and ends to the back.

Gum label: Cut one from white paper and shade the edge with brown chalk. Add the black penwork.

Gum wrapper: Cut one from mustard yellow cardstock and wrap around the aluminum foil rectangle. Shade the front corners with brown chalk.

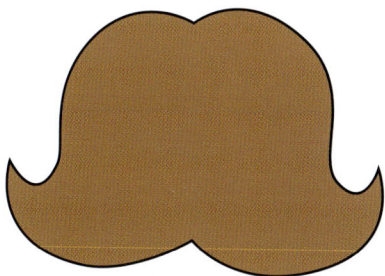

Collar: Cut one from red paper.

Headband: Cut one from red paper.

Hair: Cut one from brown paper and shade the edge with brown chalk.

Bangs: Cut one from brown paper.

Face: Cut one from ivory paper. Use the black pen to draw her mouth and eyes. Shade her cheeks with pink chalk.

Embroidery floss: Tie a ¾" bow with 1" tails. Glue it to his neck.

Ghost: Cut one from white paper and crumple up. Smooth it out and chalk the edges with brown chalk. Use the black pen to draw his eyes. Shade his cheeks with pink chalk.

who brings us so much joy

15

H

is for Horse,

ride'm cowboy!

You will need:

patterned Paper Pizazz®:
blue stars (Jacie's
Watercolor Naturals, also
available by the sheet)
solid Paper Pizazz®:
 • *navy blue, red, green,*
  light yellow, dark purple
  (Teresa's Handpicked
  Solid Jewel Tones)
 • *light tan, black, speckled*
  (Teresa's Handpicked
  Solid Muted Colors)
 • *goldenrod (Plain Brights)*

 • *white, light ivory (New*
  Plain Pastels)
decorating chalks: red, brown
2½"x4½" rectangle of
 newspaper
26-gauge brass craft wire
2"x2½" piece of black wire
 mesh
toothpick
⅛" hole punch
needle nose pliers
wire cutters
basic supplies (see page 1)

1 Cut two 5½"x8½" light yellow rectangles. Cut a 5½"x8½" piece of stars paper and tear it into two borders (see page 1). Glue one piece of stars to a yellow piece with the tears facing the inside of the spread.

2 Mat your photo on white. Mat it again on black with a torn border. Glue it centered on the left hand page.

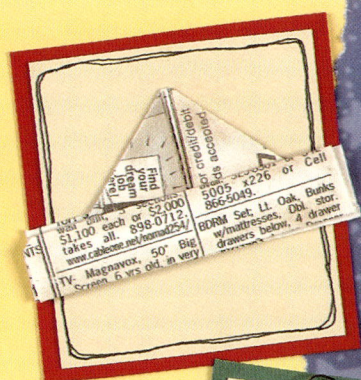

hanger

H

3 Cut out two "H" alphabet tiles and chalk the checkerboards with red. Mat each tile onto a 1¼" white square and outline them with a black wavy double border as shown. Glue one to each page. Hand write or computer print your words on white paper. Use the pen to add a black border then chalk the "H" word red. Glue them to the left hand page.

4 Cut three 2¼" tan squares. Use the black pen to outline each square with a wavy double border as shown. Mat one on red, one on green and one on navy blue, each with a ¼" border.

5 Use the patterns to cut out the hat, hanger and heart. Glue each to a tan square as shown then glue them to the right hand page.

Newspaper hat: Photocopy a newspaper of this size onto acid-free white or light ivory paper. Cut out this pattern. Fold it following the directions below, then shade the edges with brown chalk.

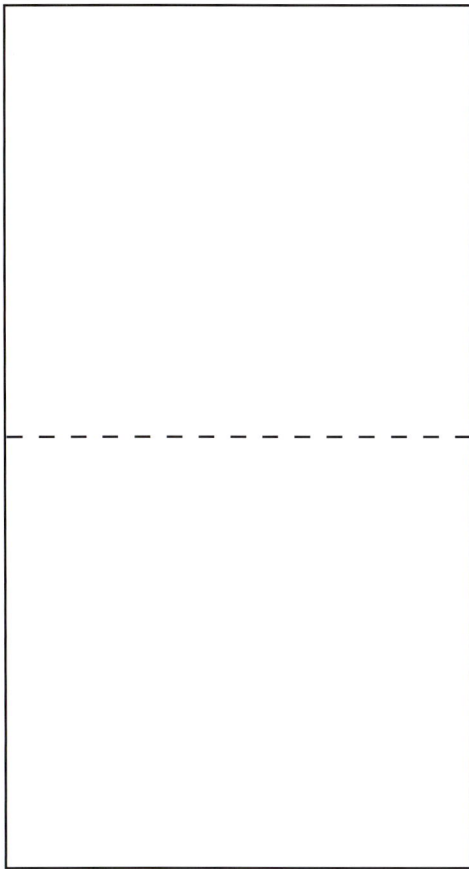

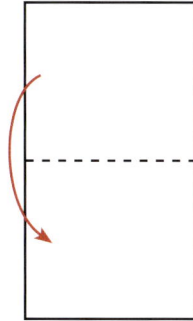

fold

Fold in half.

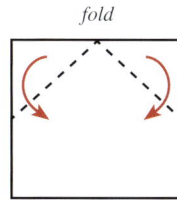

Fold each corner to the center.

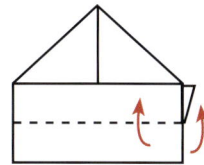

Fold each bottom flap in half upward.

Fold each bottom flap up one more time to finish.

Tabs: Cut two from goldenrod paper and fold each in half.

Hanger: Use the pattern to shape the hanger from the craft wire.

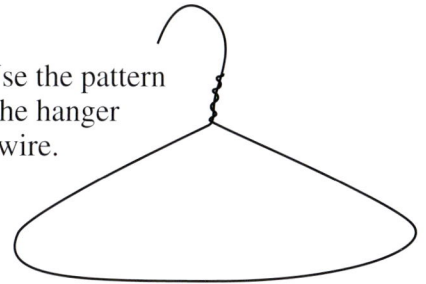

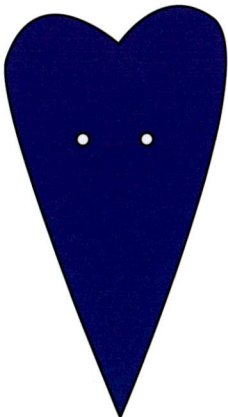

Sign: Cut one from goldenrod paper.

hanger

Sign: Cut one from white paper. Use the black pen to draw the dashed line and to write "hanger."

Square: Cut one from light ivory paper. Tear the edges and chalk them with brown.

Heart: Cut one from dark purple paper. Punch the holes as indicated. Break the tips off of the toothpick and thread it through the holes as shown in the photo.

ride'm cowboy!

17

is for Icing,

a yummy sticky mess

You will need:

patterned Paper Pizazz®: yellow gingham (Soft Tints, also available by the sheet)

solid Paper Pizazz®:
- red, green, dark green, brown (Teresa's Handpicked Solid Jewel Tones)
- light tan, light brown, sage green, blue (Teresa's Handpicked Solid Muted Colors)
- goldenrod (Plain Brights)
- white, light ivory, pink (New Plain Pastels)

decorating chalks: green, brown, black

two 2½" lengths of raffia

fine tip red pen

basic supplies (see page 1)

1 Cut two 5½"x8½" gingham rectangles. Cut a 5½"x8½" piece of sage green paper and tear it into two borders (see page 1). Glue one piece of sage green paper to a gingham piece with the tears facing the inside of the spread.

2 Mat your photo on white. Mat it again on blue with a torn border. Glue it centered on the left hand page.

3 Cut out two "I" alphabet tiles and chalk the checkerboards with green. Mat each tile onto a 1¼" white square and outline them with a black wavy double border as shown. Glue one to each page. Hand write or computer print your words on white paper. Use the pen to add a black border then chalk the "I" word green. Glue them to the left hand page.

4 Cut three 2¼" tan squares. Use the black pen to outline each square with a wavy double border as shown. Mat one on goldenrod, one on green and one on red, each with a ¼" border.

5 Use the patterns to cut out the island, ice cream cone and Indian. Glue each to a tan square as shown then glue them to the right hand page.

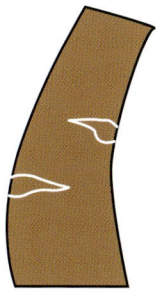

Tree trunk: Cut one from brown. Add the black penwork then shade the edges with brown chalk.

is for Icing,

Leaf: Cut four from dark green paper and shade the edge with black chalk.

Island: Cut one from light brown paper and tear the top edge. Shade the torn edge with brown chalk.

Water: Cut one from blue paper and shade the edges with black chalk.

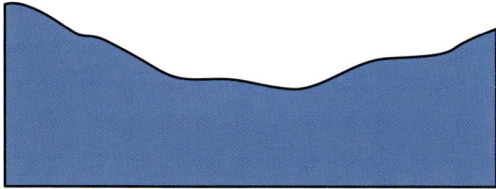

a yummy sticky mess

Ice cream scoop: Cut one from pink paper. Shade the edge with brown chalk.

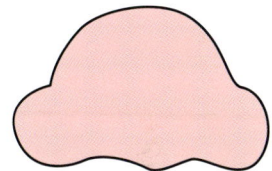

Cherry: Cut one from red paper and shade with black chalk.

Cone: Cut one from light brown paper. Add the black penwork then shade the edge with brown chalk.

Ice cream scoop: Cut one from white paper. Shade the edge with brown chalk.

Feathers: Cut one each from red, dark green and goldenrod paper. Shade the edges each with black chalk.

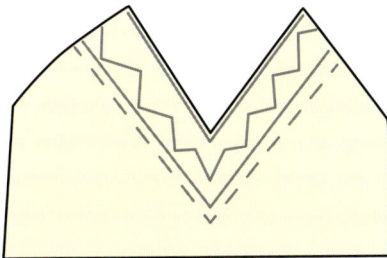

Head: Cut one from light brown paper. Add the penwork with the black pen then shade the edge with brown chalk and the cheeks with pink chalk.

Shirt and headband: Cut one of each from light ivory paper. Add the penwork with the black and red pens then shade the edges with brown chalk.

Hair: Cut one from black paper.

Braids: Cut two from black paper. Wrap the end of each with raffia and tie it in the front, trimming the ends to ¼".

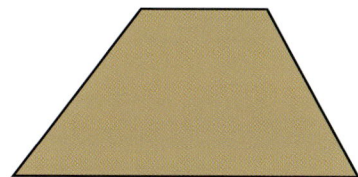

Body: Cut one from light brown paper.

J is for Jumping,

across a small crevice

You will need:

*patterned Paper Pizazz®: blue dots (Soft Tints, also
available by the sheet)*
specialty Paper Pizazz®: white vellum (Vellum Papers)
solid Paper Pizazz®:
- *navy blue, red (Teresa's Handpicked Solid Jewel
Tones)*
- *light tan, brown, orange, light purple (Teresa's
Handpicked Solid Muted Colors)*
- *goldenrod (Plain Brights)*
- *white, light ivory, pink (New Plain Pastels)*
mustard yellow cardstock
*decorating chalks: white, pink, green, brown, purple,
orange*
4" length of ivory embroidery floss
X-acto® knife, cutting surface
basic supplies (see page 1)

1 Cut two 5½"x8½" red rectangles. Cut a 5½"x8½" piece of dots paper and tear it into two borders (see page 1). Glue one piece of dots to a red piece with the tears facing the inside of the spread.

2 Mat your photo on white. Mat it again on navy blue with a torn border. Glue it centered on the left hand page.

3 Cut out two "J" alphabet tiles and chalk the checkerboards with green. Mat each tile onto a 1¼" white square and outline them with a black wavy double border as shown. Glue one to each page. Hand write or computer print your words on white paper. Use the pen to add a black border then chalk the "J" word green. Glue them to the left hand page.

4 Cut three 2¼" tan squares. Use the black pen to outline each square with a wavy double border as shown. Mat one on goldenrod, one on red and one on navy blue, each with a ¼" border.

5 Use the patterns to cut out the jelly beans, juice and Jesus. Glue each to a tan square as shown then glue them to the right hand page.

Jelly beans: Cut one from orange, two from pink and two from light purple paper. Shade the edge of the orange bean with orange chalk, the edges of the pink beans with pink chalk and the edges of the purple beans with purple chalk. Highlight each with white chalk.

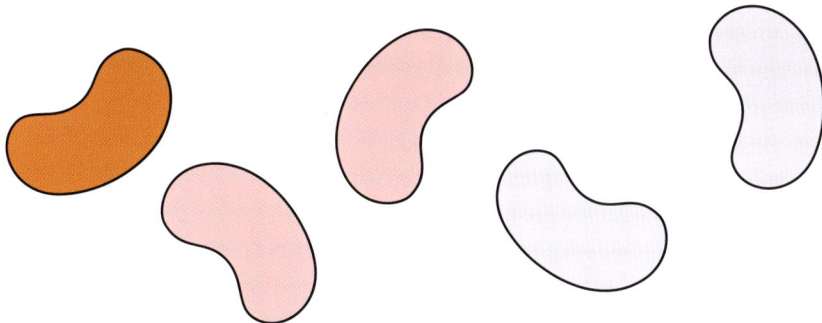

Juice: Cut one from orange paper.

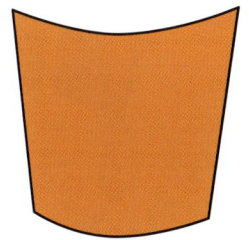

Straw: Cut one from white paper. Add the penwork.

Glass: Cut one from white vellum. Add the penwork, let dry, then cut on the dashed line with the X-acto® knife.

Jesus: Cut one from light ivory paper. Add the penwork then shade his cheeks with pink chalk.

Hay: Cut six from mustard yellow cardstock.

Manger: Cut one from brown paper and shade the edges with brown chalk.

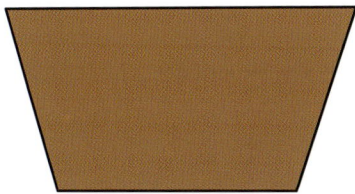

Manger legs: Cut two from brown paper and shade the edges with brown chalk.

Heart: Cut one from red paper. Add the penwork then shade the point with black chalk.

Floss: Tie a bow with ¼" loops and ½" tails then glue it at his neck.

Swaddling: Cut one from white paper and shade the edge with brown chalk.

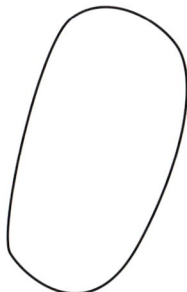

across a small crevice

K is for Kiss goodnight,

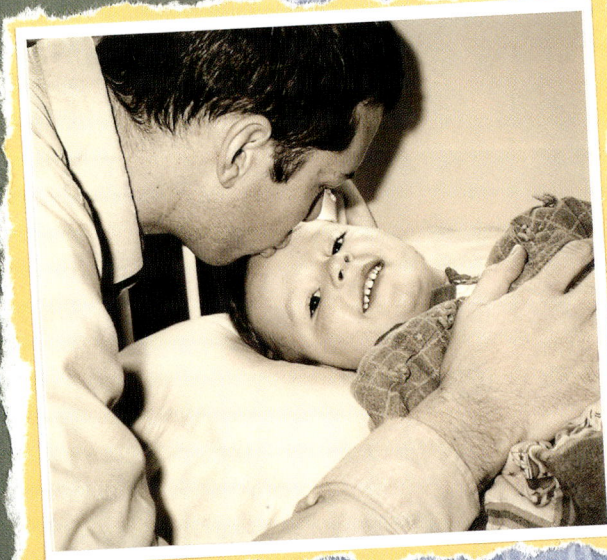

by my daddy dear

You will need:

patterned Paper Pizazz®: blue plaid (Coordinating Florals & Patterns, also available by the sheet)
solid Paper Pizazz®:
- navy blue, red, green (Teresa's Handpicked Solid Jewel Tones)
- light tan, light brown, orange, dark sage green (Teresa's Handpicked Solid Muted Colors)
- goldenrod (Plain Brights)
- white (New Plain Pastels)

decorating chalks: light blue, black, brown
mustard yellow cardstock
3" length of 24-gauge black craft wire
4" length of jute twine
three 2" lengths of raffia
1/8" hole punch
needle nose pliers
basic supplies (see page 1)

1 Cut two 5½"x8½" plaid rectangles. Cut a 5½"x8½" piece of dark sage paper and tear it into two borders (see page 1). Glue one piece of sage to a plaid piece with the tears facing the inside of the spread.

2 Mat your photo on white. Mat it again on goldenrod with a torn border. Glue it centered on the left hand page.

3 Cut out two "K" alphabet tiles and chalk the checkerboards with light blue. Mat each tile onto a 1¼" white square and outline them with a black wavy double border as shown. Glue one to each page. Hand write or computer print your words on white paper. Use the pen to add a black border then chalk the "K" word light blue. Glue them to the left hand page.

4 Cut three 2¼" tan squares. Use the black pen to outline each square with a wavy double border as shown. Mat one on green, one on goldenrod and one on navy blue, each with a ¼" border.

5 Use the patterns to cut out the keys, kite and ketchup. Glue each to a tan square as shown then glue them to the right hand page.

Keys: Cut one from orange, one from navy blue and one from mustard yellow cardstock. Punch a hole in the top of each. Shade the orange and blue keys with black chalk and the yellow key with brown chalk.

Key chain: Use the pattern to shape the wire into a coil. String the keys onto the coil.

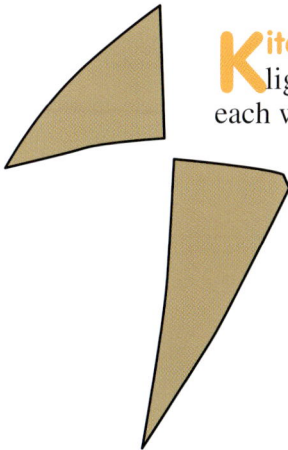

Kite: Cut one of each from light brown paper. Shade each with black chalk.

Kite: Cut one from navy blue paper. Shade the edges with black chalk.

Tail: Tie three pieces of raffia evenly spaced onto the jute, trimming the tails to ½". Glue one end of the jute to the back of the kite.

Cap: Cut one from white paper. Shade the edge with brown chalk.

by my daddy dear

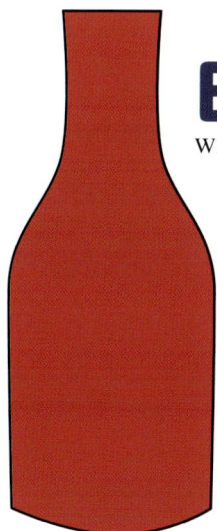

Bottle: Cut one from red paper. Shade it with black chalk.

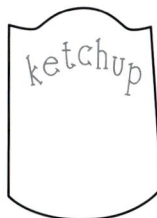

ketchup

Leaf: Cut one from green paper. Shade it with black chalk.

Label: Cut one from white paper. Add the black penwork then shade it with brown chalk.

Tomato: Cut one from red paper. Shade it with black chalk.

23

L is for Licking,

both the beaters here

You will need:
patterned Paper Pizazz®: yellow gingham (Soft Tints, also available by the sheet)
solid Paper Pizazz®:
  • *navy blue, red, green, black (Teresa's Handpicked Solid Jewel Tones)*
  • *light tan, light brown, medium blue, gray (Teresa's Handpicked Solid Muted Colors)*
  • *goldenrod (Plain Brights)*
  • *white (New Plain Pastels)*
decorating chalks: red, pink, black
white liquid appliqué (lamb's wool) or white dimensional paint
embossing heat tool or hair dryer
mini pinking pattern-edge scissors
basic supplies (see page 1)

1 Cut two 5½"x8½" navy blue rectangles. Cut a 5½"x8½" piece of gingham paper and tear it into two borders (see page 1). Glue one piece of gingham paper to a navy piece with the tears facing the inside of the spread.

2 Mat your photo on white. Mat it again on black with a torn border. Glue it centered on the left hand page.

3 Cut out two "L" alphabet tiles and chalk the checkerboards with red. Mat each tile onto a 1¼" white square and outline them with a black wavy double border as shown. Glue one to each page. Hand write or computer print your words on white paper. Use the pen to add a black border then chalk the "L" word red. Glue them to the left hand page.

4 Cut three 2¼" tan squares. Use the black pen to outline each square with a wavy double border as shown. Mat one on red, one on blue and one on green, each with a ¼" border.

5 Use the patterns to cut out the leaves, lunch sack and lamb. Glue each to a tan square as shown then glue them to the right hand page.

is for Licking,

lunch ♡

fold 2

fold 1

both the beaters here

Leaves: Cut one of each from red, goldenrod and green paper. Shade the edges and veins of each leaf with black chalk.

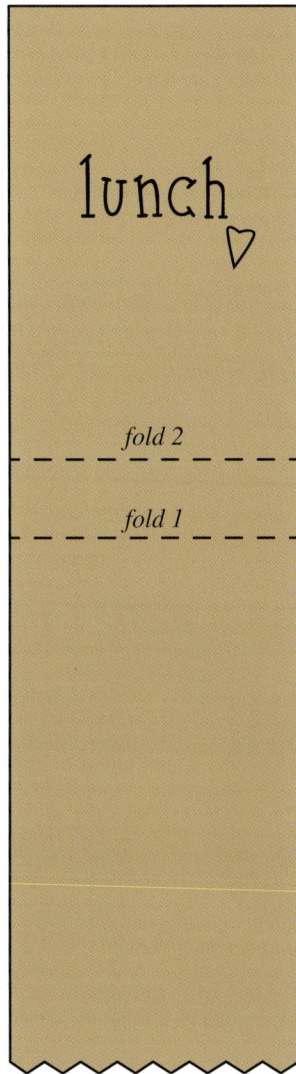

Lunch sack: Cut one from light brown paper, trimming the bottom edge with the pinking scissors. Fold it in half on Fold 1. Fold both layers together on Fold 2. Add the penwork then chalk the edges with black chalk and the heart with red chalk.

Hair: Cut one from gray paper. Follow the manufacturer's directions to apply liquid appliqué and set it with the heat tool. Or, apply dimensional paint.

Head: Cut one from gray paper. Add the penwork with the black pen then shade the edge with black chalk and the cheeks with pink chalk.

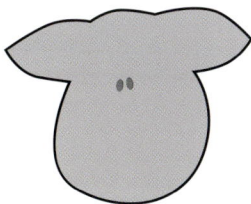

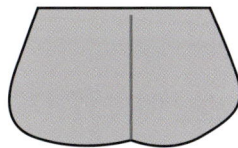

Legs: Cut one from gray paper. Add the penwork with the black pen then shade the edge with black chalk.

Body: Cut one from gray paper. Follow the manufacturer's directions to apply liquid appliqué and set it with the heat tool. Or, apply dimensional paint.

M is for Motorcycle,

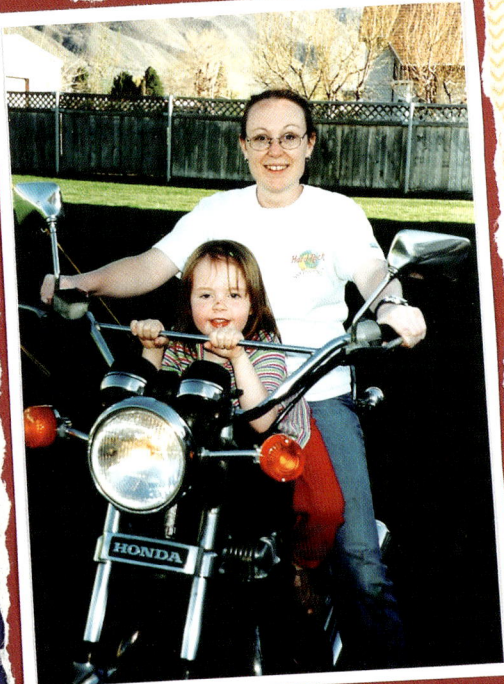

vroom! vroom! vroooom!

You will need:
patterned Paper Pizazz®: yellow squiggle (Soft Tints)
specialty Paper Pizazz®: white vellum (Vellum Papers)
solid Paper Pizazz®:
  • *navy blue, red, green, yellow (Teresa's Handpicked Solid Jewel Tones)*
  • *light tan, light brown, brown, olive green (Teresa's Handpicked Solid Muted Colors)*
  • *goldenrod (Plain Brights)*
  • *white, light yellow (New Plain Pastels)*
decorating chalks: red, black, brown
⅛" brown brad
X-acto® knife, cutting surface
basic supplies (see page 1)

1 Cut two 5½"x8½" yellow squiggle rectangles. Cut a 5½"x8½" piece of navy blue paper and tear it into two borders (see page 1). Glue one piece of navy to a squiggle piece with the tears facing the inside of the spread.

2 Mat your photo on white. Mat it again on red with a torn border. Glue it centered on the left hand page.

3 Cut out two "M" alphabet tiles and chalk the checkerboards with red. Mat each tile onto a 1¼" white square and outline them with a black wavy double border as shown. Glue one to each page. Hand write or computer print your words on white paper. Use the pen to add a black border then chalk the "M" word red. Glue them to the left hand page.

4 Cut three 2¼" tan squares. Use the black pen to outline each square with a wavy double border as shown. Mat one on goldenrod, one on red and one on green, each with a ¼" border.

5 Use the patterns to cut out the magnifying glass, mosquito, monkey, moon and star. Glue each to a tan square as shown then glue them to the right hand page.

is for Motorcycle,

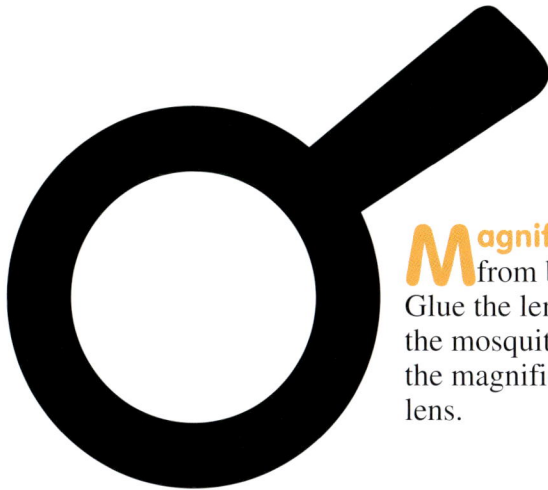

Magnifier: Cut one from black paper. Glue the lens circle over the mosquito circle. Glue the magnifier over the lens.

Lens: Cut one from white vellum

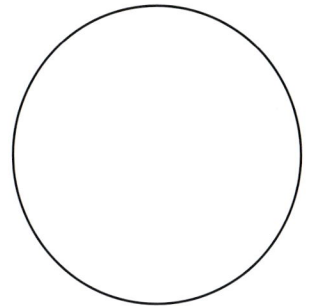

Grip: Cut one from olive green paper. Add the black penwork.

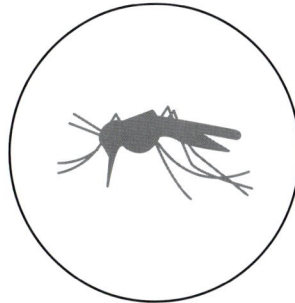

Mosquito circle: Cut one circle from white vellum, place it over the mosquito and draw the mosquito with the black pen.

Eyes: Cut one from white paper. Draw the eyes with the black pen.

Tummy: Cut one from light brown paper. Shade the edge with brown chalk.

Mouth: Cut one from light brown paper. Draw the nose and mouth with the black pen.

Moon: Cut one from goldenrod paper. Crumple it up and smooth it out. Shade the edge with brown and black chalk.

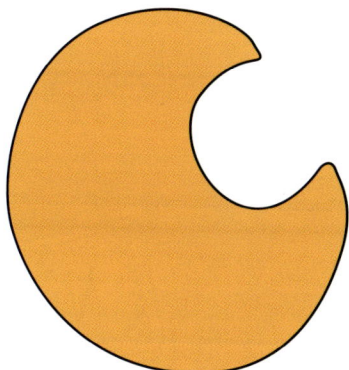

Body: Cut one from brown paper. Shade the edge with brown chalk.

Star: Cut one from light yellow paper and shade the edge with brown chalk. Attach it to the light tan mat with the brad.

vroom! vroom! vroooom!

27

N is for Napping baby,

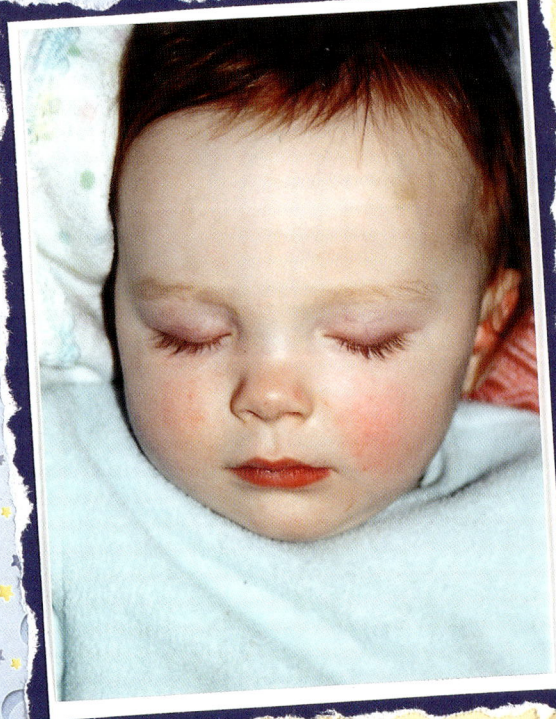

in the afternoon

You will need:

patterned Paper Pizazz®: moons & stars (Mixing Baby Papers, also available by the sheet)
solid Paper Pizazz®:
- navy blue, red (Teresa's Handpicked Solid Jewel Tones)
- light tan, light brown (Teresa's Handpicked Solid Muted Colors)
- goldenrod (Plain Brights)

- white, ivory, light yellow (New Plain Pastels)
decorating chalks: light blue, brown, black, pink
9" length of 26-gauge silver craft wire
4" square of black wire mesh
2¼"x2¾" rectangle of newspaper
broken red rubber band
needle nose pliers
basic supplies (see page 1)

1 Cut two 5½"x8½" light yellow rectangles. Cut a 5½"x8½" piece of moons & stars paper and tear it into two borders (see page 1). Glue one piece of moons & stars to a yellow piece with the tears facing the inside of the spread.

2 Mat your photo on white. Mat it again on navy blue with a torn border. Glue it centered on the left hand page.

3 Cut out two "N" alphabet tiles and chalk the checkerboards with light blue. Mat each tile onto a 1¼" white square and outline them with a black wavy double border as shown. Glue one to each page. Hand write or computer print your words on white paper. Use the pen to add a black border then chalk the "N" word light blue. Glue them to the left hand page.

4 Cut three 2¼" tan squares. Use the black pen to outline each square with a wavy double border as shown. Mat one on navy blue, one on goldenrod and one on red, each with a ¼" border.

5 Use the patterns to cut out the net, nurse and newspaper. Glue each to a tan square as shown then glue them to the right hand page.

Fish: Cut one from light brown paper. Add the black penwork then shade it with brown chalk.

Net: Cut one circle from the mesh. Thread the wire in and out around the edge to gather. Fold one end of the remaining wire to make a handle. Then wrap the other end around the handle base 6-8 times as shown in the photo on page 28.

Bangs: Cut one from goldenrod paper and shade the edge with brown chalk.

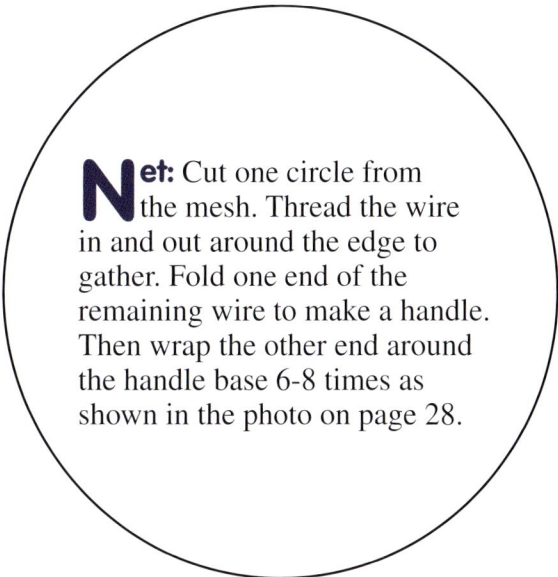

Cross: Cut one from red paper and shade the edges with black chalk.

Hat: Cut one from white paper and shade the edge with brown chalk.

Hair: Cut one from goldenrod paper and shade the edge with brown chalk.

Face: Cut one from ivory paper. Add the black penwork. Shade the cheeks with pink chalk.

Neck: Cut one from ivory paper.

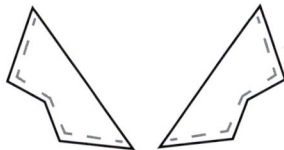

Newspaper: Photocopy a newspaper of this size onto acid-free white paper. Cut out the pattern. Roll it up, tie it with the rubber band and shade the edge with brown chalk.

Collar: Cut one of each from white paper. Add the black penwork and shade the edges with brown chalk.

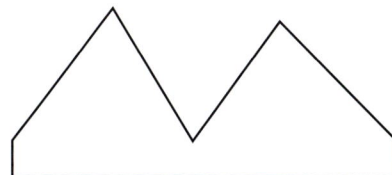

Uniform: Cut one from white paper and shade the edge with brown chalk.

O is for Outside,

where I love to be

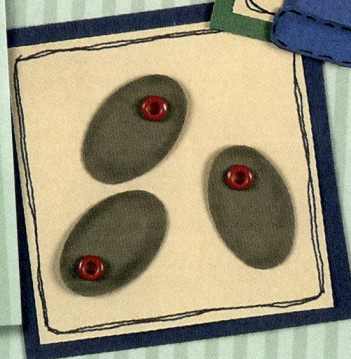

You will need:

patterned Paper Pizazz®: green
  stripes (Soft Tints, also available
  by the sheet)
solid Paper Pizazz®:
  • navy blue, dark blue, red, green
    (Teresa's Handpicked Solid
    Jewel Tones)
  • light tan, medium blue, light
    brown, blue, olive green
    (Teresa's Handpicked Solid
    Muted Colors)
  • white, light yellow (New Plain
    Pastels)
decorating chalks: green, brown,
  black
two ⅛" nickel brads
three ⅛" dark red eyelets
eyelet setting tools
basic supplies (see page 1)

1 Cut two 5½"x8½" stripes rectangles. Cut a 5½"x8½" piece of light yellow paper and tear it into two borders (see page 1). Glue one piece of yellow paper to a stripes piece with the tears facing the inside of the spread.

2 Mat your photo on white. Mat it again on medium blue with a torn border. Glue it centered on the left hand page.

3 Cut out two "O" alphabet tiles and chalk the checkerboards with green. Mat each tile onto a 1¼" white square and outline them with a black wavy double border as shown. Glue one to each page. Hand write or computer print your words on white paper. Use the pen to add a black border then chalk the "O" word green. Glue them to the left hand page.

4 Cut three 2¼" tan squares. Use the black pen to outline each square with a wavy double border as shown. Mat one on red, one on green and one on navy blue, each with a ¼" border.

5 Use the patterns to cut out the oars, overalls and olives. Glue each to a tan square then glue them to the right hand page.

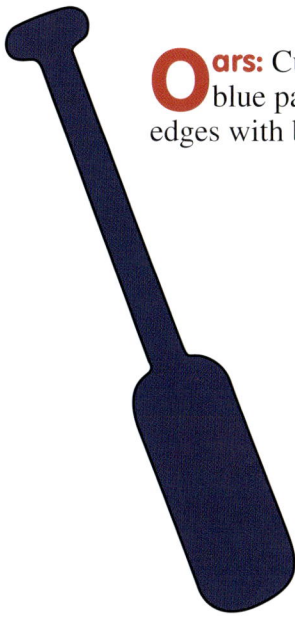

Oars: Cut two from navy blue paper and shade the edges with black chalk.

Oar tips: Cut two from light brown paper and shade the edges with brown chalk.

Chest pocket: Cut one from dark blue paper. Add the black penwork then shade the edge with black chalk.

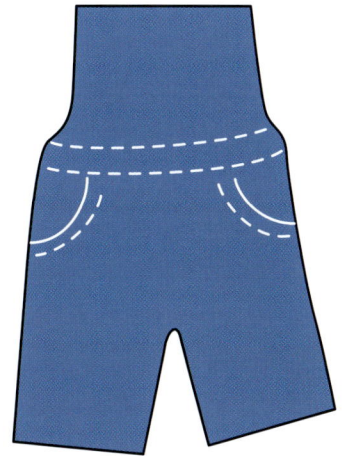

Side pocket: Cut one from dark blue paper. Add the black penwork then shade the edge with black chalk.

Overalls: Cut one from dark blue paper. Add the black penwork then shade the edge with black chalk.

Straps: Cut two from dark blue paper. Add the black penwork then shade the edges with black chalk. Attach the straps with the brads.

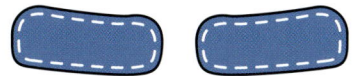

where I love to be

Pant cuffs: Cut one of each from dark blue paper. Add the black penwork then shade the edges with black chalk.

Olives: Cut three from olive green paper. Attach an eyelet (see page 1) in one end of each olive.

P is for Planting Peas,

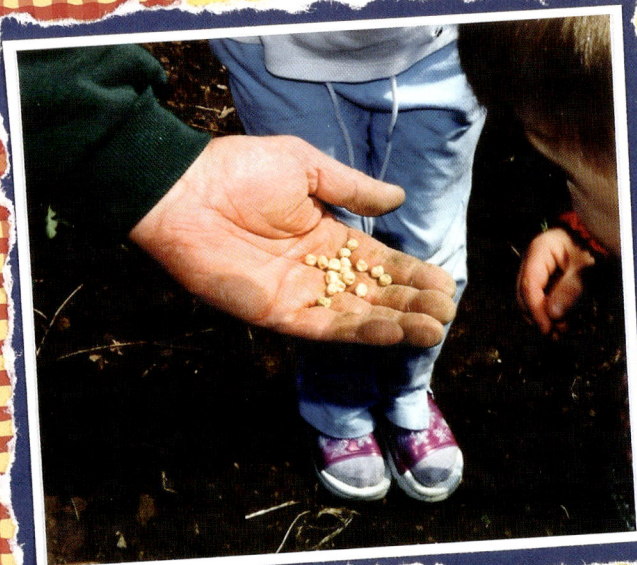

just Grandpa and me

You will need:
patterned Paper Pizazz®: red & yellow gingham (Bright Tints)
solid Paper Pizazz®:
• navy blue, red, green, yellow, brown (Teresa's Handpicked Solid Jewel Tones)
• light tan, light brown, orange, black (Teresa's Handpicked Solid Muted Colors)
• goldenrod (Plain Brights)
• white, pink (New Plain Pastels)
mustard yellow cardstock
decorating chalks: red, yellow, brown
two 2" lengths of 26-gauge black craft wire
white liquid appliqué or white dimensional paint
embossing heat tool or hair dryer
needle nose pliers
X-acto® knife, cutting surface
basic supplies (see page 1)

1 Cut two 5½"x8½" yellow rectangles. Cut a 5½"x8½" piece of gingham paper and tear it into two borders (see page 1). Glue one piece of gingham to a yellow piece with the tears facing the inside of the spread.

2 Mat your photo on white. Mat it again on navy blue with a torn border. Glue it centered on the left hand page.

3 Cut out two "P" alphabet tiles and chalk the checkerboards with red. Mat each tile onto a 1¼" white square and outline them with a black wavy double border as shown. Glue one to each page. Hand write or computer print your words on white paper. Use the pen to add a black border then chalk the "P" word red. Glue them to the left hand page.

4 Cut three 2¼" tan squares. Use the black pen to outline each square with a wavy double border as shown. Mat one on green, one on goldenrod and one on navy blue, each with a ¼" border.

5 Use the patterns to cut out the pencil, popcorn, box and pumpkin. Glue each to a tan square as shown then glue them to the right hand page.

Lead: Cut one from black paper.

Tip: Cut one from white paper. Shade the edges with brown chalk.

No 2

Label: Cut one from white paper. Add the black penwork and shade each end with brown chalk.

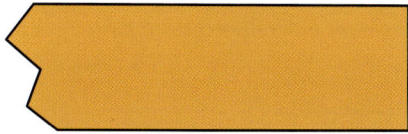

Pencil: Cut one from mustard yellow cardstock. Shade it with brown chalk.

Rim: Cut one from light brown paper. Shade the edge with brown chalk.

Eraser: Cut one from pink paper. Shade the edge with brown chalk.

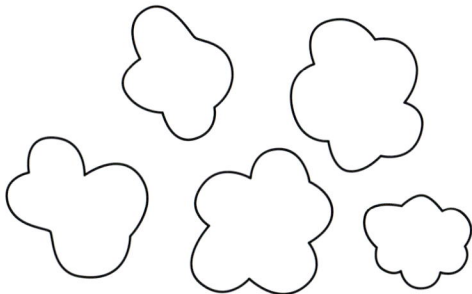

Popcorn: Cut one of each from white paper. Follow the manufacturer's directions to apply liquid appliqué to each and set with the heat tool or apply dimensional paint to each piece. "Butter" each piece with yellow chalk.

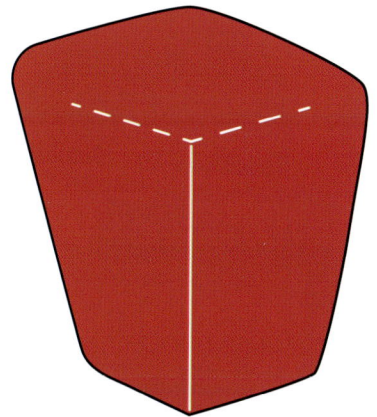

just Grandpa and me

Box: Cut one from red paper. Cut along the dashed line with the X-acto® knife and make a fold along the solid line to form a crease. Shade the edges and the solid line with brown chalk.

Leaf: Tear one from green paper.

Stem: Tear one from brown paper then crumple it up and smooth it out.

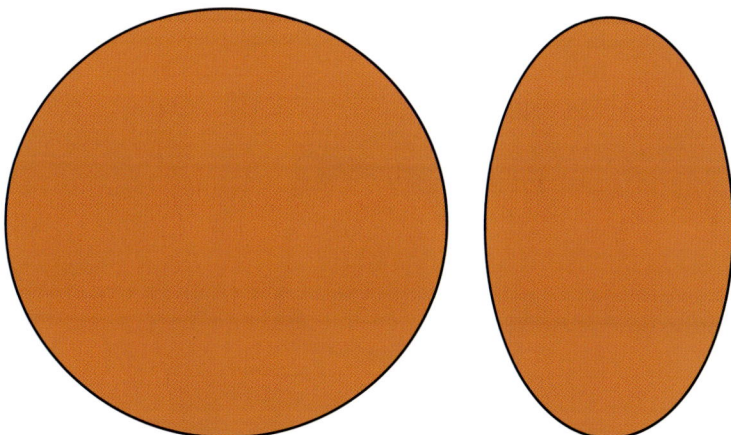

Vines: Use the patterns to shape one of each from black wire with the pliers.

Pumpkin: Tear one of each from orange paper. Crumple up and smooth it out. Shade the edges with brown chalk.

is for Quartet,

together cousins play

You will need:

patterned Paper Pizazz®: stars on yellow
   (available by the sheet)
solid Paper Pizazz®:
   • navy blue, red, green (Teresa's Handpicked
     Solid Jewel Tones)
   • orange, light tan, sage green (Teresa's
     Handpicked Solid Muted Colors)
   • goldenrod (Plain Brights)
   • white, ivory (New Plain Pastels)
1¾"x2⅝" rectangle of cardboard
decorating chalks: green, brown, black
cotton fabric: brown, red/brown gingham, green/
   brown gingham, red/yellow/green plaid
quarter
2" length of jute twine
basic supplies (see page 1)

1 Cut two 5½"x8½" stars on yellow rectangles. Cut a 5½"x8½" piece of navy blue paper and tear it into two borders (see page 1). Glue one piece of navy to a stars piece with the tears facing the inside of the spread.

2 Mat your photo on white. Mat it again on sage green with a torn border. Glue it centered on the left hand page.

3 Cut out two "Q" alphabet tiles and chalk the checkerboards with green. Mat each tile onto a 1¼" white square and outline them with a black wavy double border as shown. Glue one to each page. Hand write or computer print your words on white paper. Use the pen to add a black border then chalk the "Q" word green. Glue them to the left hand page.

4 Cut three 2¼" tan squares. Use the black pen to outline each square with a wavy double border as shown. Mat one on green, one on goldenrod and one on red, each with a ¼" border.

5 Use the patterns to cut out the question mark, quilt pieces and papers for the quarter. Glue each to a tan square as shown then glue them to the right hand page.

is for Quartet,

Question mark: Cut one of each from orange paper. Shade the edges with black chalk.

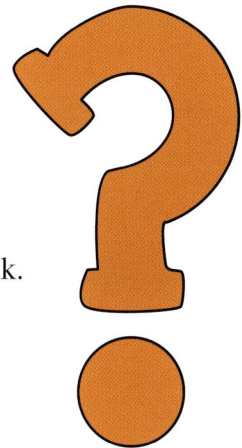

Quilt background: Cut one 3"x2" rectangle from brown fabric. Place it over the cardboard rectangle and wrap each edge under and secure with glue.

Quilt squares: Cut four ⅝" squares from each fabric. Glue them to the brown fabric as shown in the photo on page 34.

together cousins play

Jute: Knot the center of the length and glue it to the light tan mat above the quarter.

Quarter: Tear one 1¾" square from navy blue paper.

Quarter: Tear one ⅝" square from red paper and shade the edges with black chalk.

Quarter: Tear one 1½" circle from ivory paper and shade it with brown chalk.

R is for Railroad tracks,

on a lazy day

R

You will need:

patterned Paper Pizazz®:
  *green swirls (Soft Tints, also
  available by the sheet)*
solid Paper Pizazz®:
  • *navy blue, red (Teresa's
    Handpicked Solid Jewel
    Tones)*
  • *light tan, gray, blue,
    dark gray-blue (Teresa's
    Handpicked Solid Muted
    Colors)*
  • *goldenrod (Plain Brights)*
  • *white (New Plain Pastels)*
mustard yellow cardstock
*decorating chalks: red, brown,
  black*
10" length of jute twine
tacky craft glue
basic supplies (see page 1)

1 Cut two 5½"x8½" gray-blue rectangles. Cut a 5½"x8½" piece of swirls paper and tear it into two borders (see page 1). Glue one piece of swirls paper to a gray-blue piece with the tears facing the inside of the spread.

2 Mat your photo on white. Mat it again on red with a torn border. Glue it centered on the left hand page.

3 Cut out two "R" alphabet tiles and chalk the checkerboards with red. Mat each tile onto a 1¼" white square and outline them with a black wavy double border as shown. Glue one to each page. Hand write or computer print your words on white paper. Use the pen to add a black border then chalk the "R" word red. Glue them to the left hand page.

4 Cut three 2¼" tan squares. Use the black pen to outline each square with a wavy double border as shown. Mat one on goldenrod, one on navy blue and one on red, each with a ¼" border.

5 Use the patterns to cut out the rain cloud, raindrops and rooster. Glue each to a tan square as shown then glue them to the right hand page.

Cloud: Cut one from gray paper and shade the edge with black chalk.

Raindrops: Cut five from blue paper.

Beak: Cut one from mustard yellow cardstock and shade with the brown chalk.

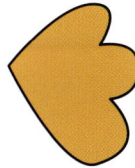

Cockscomb: Cut four from red paper. Shade each with black chalk.

Wing: Cut one from mustard yellow cardstock and shade the edge with brown chalk.

Rooster: Cut one from mustard yellow cardstock and add the black penwork after gluing the rooster to the light tan square. Shade the edge

on a lazy day

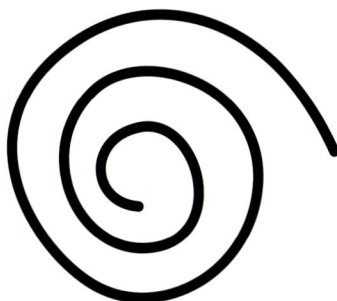

Rope: Use the pattern to draw a spiral with glue on the light tan square. Cover the glue with the twine.

S is for **Secret,**

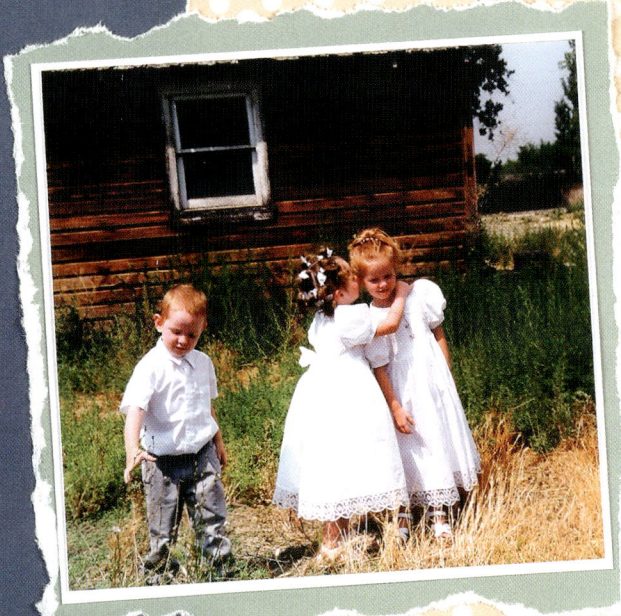

I whisper in your ear

You will need:
patterned *Paper Pizazz*®: *yellow dots (Soft Tints, also available by the sheet)*
solid *Paper Pizazz*®:
- *navy blue, red, green, brown (Teresa's Handpicked Solid Jewel Tones)*
- *light tan, sage green, dark gray-blue (Teresa's Handpicked Solid Muted Colors)*
- *goldenrod (Plain Brights)*
- *white, light ivory (New Plain Pastels)*
decorating chalks: green, brown, black
ivory embroidery floss
sewing needle
jute twine
six ⅛" silver eyelets
eyelet setting tools
optional: ¼" star punch
basic supplies (see page 1)

1 Cut two 5½"x8½" yellow dot rectangles. Cut a 5½"x8½" piece of gray-blue paper and tear it into two borders (see page 1). Glue one piece of gray-blue to a dots piece with the tears facing the inside of the spread.

2 Mat your photo on white. Mat it again on sage green with a torn border. Glue it centered on the left hand page.

3 Cut out two "S" alphabet tiles and chalk the checkerboards with green. Mat each tile onto a 1¼" white square and outline them with a black wavy double border as shown. Glue one to each page. Hand write or computer print your words on white paper. Use the pen to add a black border then chalk the "S" word green. Glue them to the left hand page.

4 Cut three 2¼" tan squares. Use the black pen to outline each square with a wavy double border as shown. Mat one on green, one on navy blue and one on goldenrod, each with a ¼" border.

5 Use the patterns to cut out the sailboat, sign and star. Glue each to a tan square as shown then glue them to the right hand page.

spiders, snails & slugs for sale!

Star: Cut one from goldenrod paper and shade the edges with black chalk. Or, use the star punch.

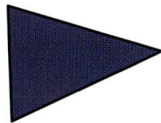

Flag: Cut one from navy blue paper and shade the edges with black chalk.

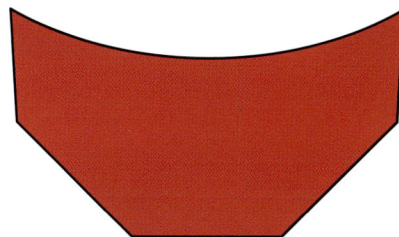

Hull: Cut one from red paper and shade the edges with black chalk.

Eyelets & jute: Attach the eyelets (see page 1) in the sails and hull as shown in the photo on page 38. Thread the jute through the eyelets and knot the ends.

Sails: Cut one of each from light ivory paper and shade the edges with brown chalk.

Mast: Cut one from brown paper.

Sign board: Cut one from brown paper and shade the edges with black chalk.

Sign post: Cut one from brown paper and shade the edges with black chalk.

spiders, snails & slugs for sale!

Sign: Cut one from light ivory paper and add the black penwork. Shade the edges with brown chalk.

Star: Cut one from navy blue and one from goldenrod paper. Shade the edges of each half with black chalk. Use the embroidery floss to sew them to the light tan square.

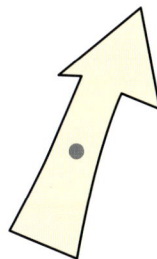

Arrow: Cut one from light ivory paper and shade the edge with brown and black chalk. Add the black penwork.

I whisper in your ear

T is for Tooth,

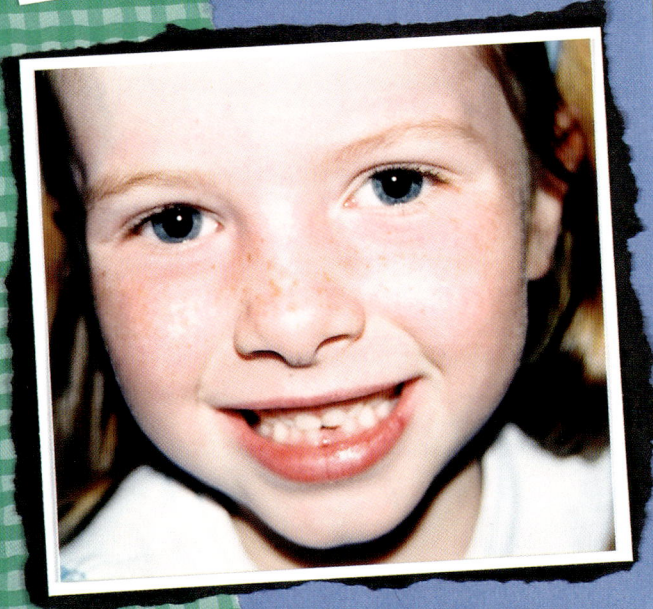

I lost my first this year!

You will need:

*patterned Paper Pizazz®: green gingham (Bright Tints, also
    available by the sheet)*
solid Paper Pizazz®:
  • *navy blue, red, green, dark green, dark purple, brown
    (Teresa's Handpicked Solid Jewel Tones)*
  • *light tan, medium blue, black (Teresa's Handpicked
    Solid Muted Colors)*
  • *white, ivory (New Plain Pastels)*
decorating chalks: light blue, red, brown, black, white
6" length of jute twine
3" length of red embroidery floss
white liquid appliqué or white dimensional paint
embossing heat tool or hair dryer
1/8" hole punch
basic supplies (see page 1)

1 Cut two 5½"x8½" medium blue rectangles.
Cut a 5½"x8½" piece of green gingham
paper and tear it into two borders (see page 1).
Glue one piece of gingham to a blue piece with
the tears facing the inside of the spread.

2 Mat your photo on white. Mat it again on black
with a torn border. Glue it centered on the left
hand page.

3 Cut out two "T" alphabet tiles and chalk the
checkerboards with red. Mat each tile onto a
1¼" white square and outline them with a black
wavy double border as shown. Glue one to each
page. Hand write or computer print your words on
white paper. Use the pen to add a black border
then chalk the "T" word red. Glue them to the left
hand page.

4 Cut three 2¼" tan squares. Use the black pen
to outline each square with a wavy double
border as shown. Mat one on navy blue, one on
red and one on green, each with a ¼" border.

5 Use the patterns to cut out the tag, tree, tire,
toothbrush and toothpaste. Glue each to a
tan square as shown then glue them to the right
hand page.

T

40

Tag: Cut one from ivory paper and punch the hole at the top. Add the black penwork then shade the edges the brown and black chalk. Loop the floss through the hole (see page 11).

Trunk: Cut one from brown paper.

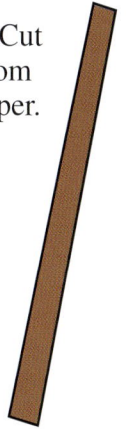

Tree: Cut one of each from dark green paper. Shade the tips with black chalk.

Tire: Cut one from black paper and shade the top left with white chalk.

Rope: Tie the jute around the tire. Glue the loose end to the back of the page.

Bristles: Cut one from white paper. Cut along the dashed lines.

Toothpaste: Cut one from white paper. Follow the manufacturer's directions to apply liquid appliqué and set with the heat tool or apply dimensional paint. Shade with light blue chalk.

Handle: Cut one from dark purple paper. Shade the edge with black chalk and the tip with white chalk.

Grip: Cut one from white paper and add the black penwork. Shade it with brown chalk.

I lost my first this year!

U is for Upside-down,

look and see my trick

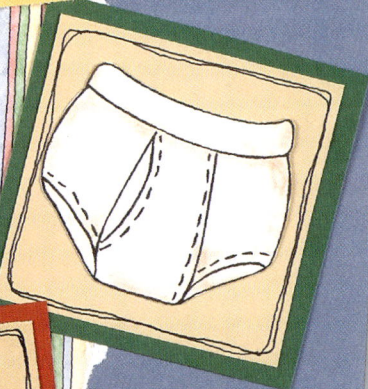

You will need:

patterned Paper Pizazz®:
 multi-color stripe (by the sheet)
solid Paper Pizazz®:
 • *navy blue, red, green, dark green, brown (Teresa's Handpicked Solid Jewel Tones)*
 • *light tan, orange, gray, medium blue (Teresa's Handpicked Solid Muted Colors)*
 • *goldenrod (Plain Brights)*
 • *white, ivory (New Plain Pastels)*
mustard yellow cardstock
decorating chalks: green, pink, brown, black
basic supplies (see page 1)

1 Cut two 5½"x8½" striped rectangles. Cut a 5½"x8½" piece of blue paper and tear it into two borders (see page 1). Glue one piece of blue paper to a striped piece with the tears facing the inside of the spread.

2 Mat your photo on white. Mat it again on goldenrod with a torn border. Glue it centered on the left hand page.

3 Cut out two "U" alphabet tiles and chalk the checkerboards with green. Mat each tile onto a 1¼" white square and outline them with a black wavy double border as shown. Glue one to each page. Hand write or computer print your words on white paper. Use the pen to add a black border then chalk the "U" word green. Glue them to the left hand page.

4 Cut three 2¼" tan squares. Use the black pen to outline each square with a wavy double border as shown. Mat one on goldenrod, one on green and one on red, each with a ¼" border.

5 Use the patterns to cut out the umbrella, underpants and upside-down boy. Glue each to a tan square as shown then glue them to the right hand page.

Stem: Cut one from gray paper and shade the edge with black chalk.

Handle: Cut one from orange paper and shade the edge with black chalk.

Umbrella: Cut one from dark green paper and shade the edge with black chalk.

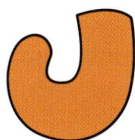

Umbrella: Cut one from orange paper and add the black penwork. Shade the bottom edge with black chalk.

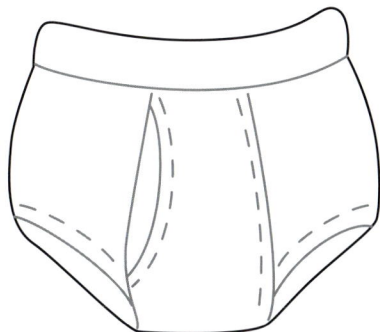

Underpants: Cut one from white paper and add the black penwork. Shade with brown chalk.

look and see my trick

Shirt stripe : Cut one from mustard yellow cardstock and add the black penwork. Shade the edges with black chalk.

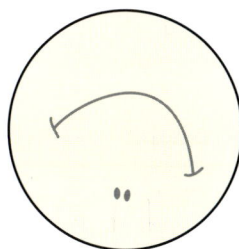

Shirt: Cut one from navy blue paper and shade the edge with black chalk. Add the black penwork after gluing the boy to the light tan square.

Face: Cut one from ivory paper and add the black penwork. Shade the cheeks with pink chalk.

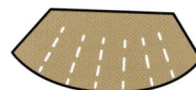

Hair: Cut one from brown paper. Cut along the dashed lines.

V is for Veterinarian,

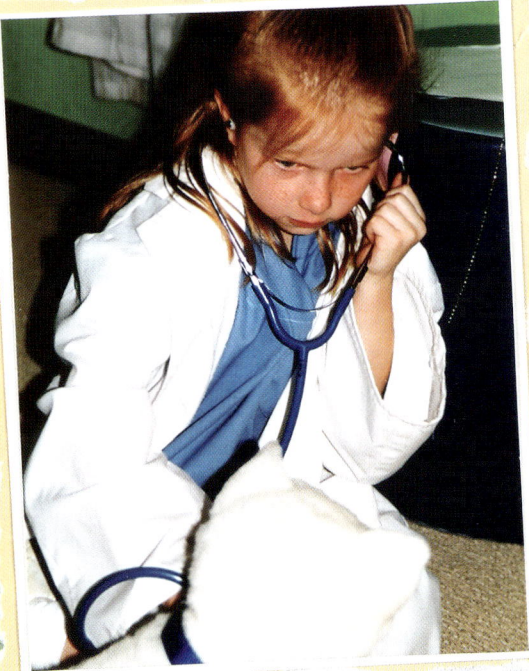

caring for the sick

You will need:
patterned Paper Pizazz®: green diamonds (Soft Tints, also available by the sheet)
solid Paper Pizazz®:
- navy blue, red, brown (Teresa's Handpicked Solid Jewel Tones)
- light tan, light brown, gray (Teresa's Handpicked Solid Muted Colors)
- goldenrod (Plain Brights)
- white, pink, lavender, light yellow (New Plain Pastels)
decorating chalks: green, brown, black
mini-scallop pattern-edge scissors
basic supplies (see page 1)

1 Cut two 5½"x8½" navy blue rectangles. Cut a 5½"x8½" piece of green diamonds paper and tear it into two borders horizontally (see page 1). Glue one piece of diamonds to a navy piece with the tears facing the inside of the spread.

2 Mat your photo on white. Mat it again on light yellow with a torn border. Glue it centered on the left hand page.

3 Cut out two "V" alphabet tiles and chalk the checkerboards with green. Mat each tile onto a 1¼" white square and outline them with a black wavy double border as shown. Glue one to each page. Hand write or computer print your words on white paper. Use the pen to add a black border then chalk the "V" word green. Glue them to the left hand page.

4 Cut three 2¼" tan squares. Use the black pen to outline each square with a wavy double border as shown. Mat one on red, one on navy blue and one on goldenrod, each with a ¼" border.

5 Use the patterns to cut out the volleyball, valentine and volcano. Glue each to a tan square as shown then glue them to the right hand page.

be mine!

Volleyball: Cut one from white paper and add the black penwork. Shade with brown chalk.

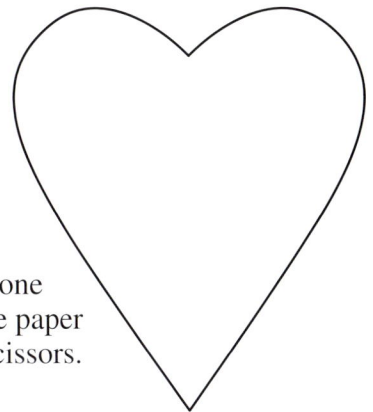

Heart: Cut one from white paper using scallop scissors.

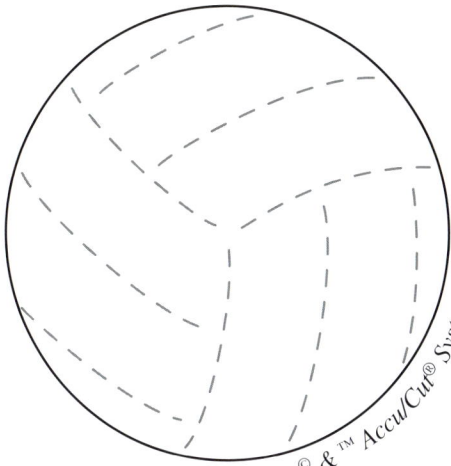

© & ™ AccuCut® Systems

Heart: Cut one from white paper and add the black penwork. Shade the edge with brown chalk.

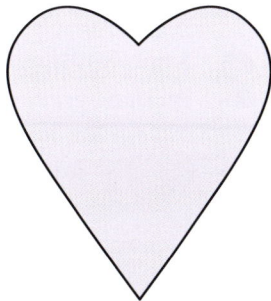

Heart: Cut one from pink paper and add the black penwork. Shade the edge with brown chalk.

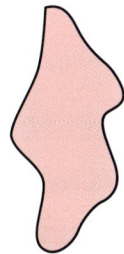

be mine!

Heart: Cut one from lavender paper.

Lava: Cut one from red paper.

Lava: Cut one from pink paper.

Smoke: Cut one from gray paper and shade with black chalk.

Mountain top: Cut one from light brown paper and shade with brown chalk.

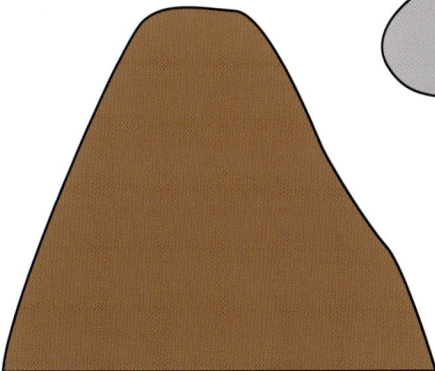

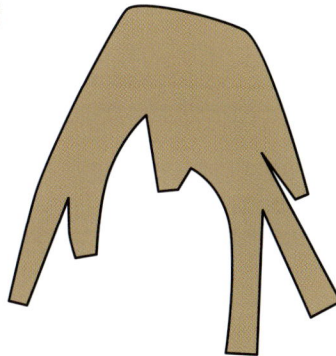

Mountain: Cut one from brown paper and shade with black chalk.

W is for Watermelon,

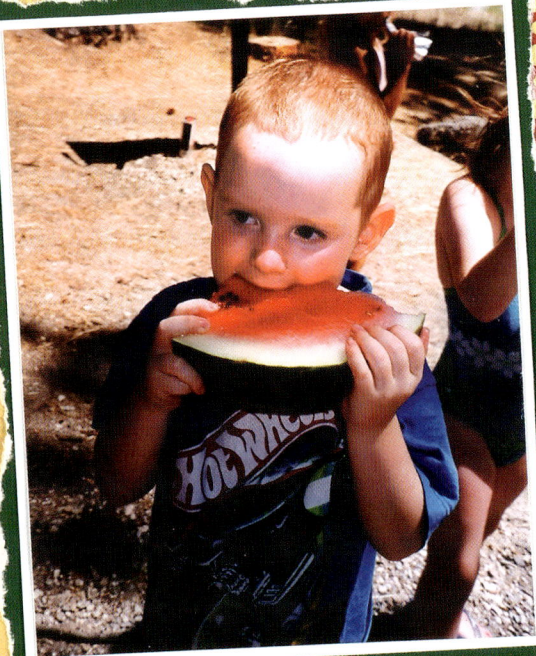

dripping off my chin

You will need:

patterned Paper Pizazz®: yellow dots on red (Bright Tints, also available by the sheet)

specialty Paper Pizazz®: white vellum (Vellum Papers)

solid Paper Pizazz®:
- navy blue, red, brown, green, dark green, (Teresa's Handpicked Solid Jewel Tones)
- light tan, light brown, olive green, yellow (Teresa's Handpicked Solid Muted Colors)
- goldenrod (Plain Brights)
- white (New Plain Pastels)

decorating chalks: green, brown, black

⅛" black brad

⅛" hole punch

white gel pen

basic supplies (see page 1)

1 Cut two 5½"x8½" yellow dots rectangles. Cut a 5½"x8½" piece of yellow paper and tear it into two borders (see page 1). Glue one piece of yellow to a dots piece with the tears facing the inside of the spread.

2 Mat your photo on white. Mat it again on dark green with a torn border. Glue it centered on the left hand page.

3 Cut out two "W" alphabet tiles and chalk the checkerboards with green. Mat each tile onto a 1¼" white square and outline them with a black wavy double border as shown. Glue one to each page. Hand write or computer print your words on white paper. Use the pen to add a black border then chalk the "W" word green. Glue them to the left hand page.

4 Cut three 2¼" tan squares. Use the black pen to outline each square with a wavy double border as shown. Mat one on green, one on red and one on navy blue, each with a ¼" border.

5 Use the patterns to cut out the watch, worm, dirt and window. Glue each to a tan square as shown then glue them to the right hand page.

Watchband: Cut one of each from brown paper. Punch the ⅛" holes. Add the white penwork then shade the edges with black chalk.

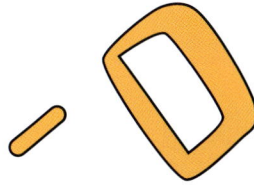

Buckle: Cut one of each from goldenrod paper. Shade the edges with black chalk.

Frame: Cut one from olive green paper. Shade the edge with black chalk.

Dirt: Cut one of each from light brown paper. Tear the top edge of each and shade with brown chalk.

Face: Cut one from white paper. Add the black penwork then shade the edge with brown chalk. Attach to the watch frame and band with the brad.

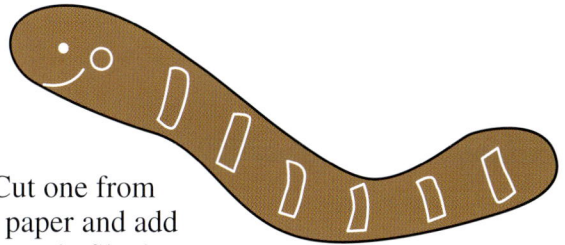

Worm: Cut one from brown paper and add the black penwork. Shade with black chalk.

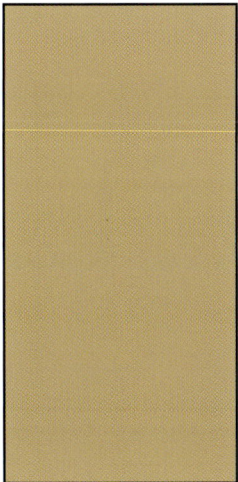

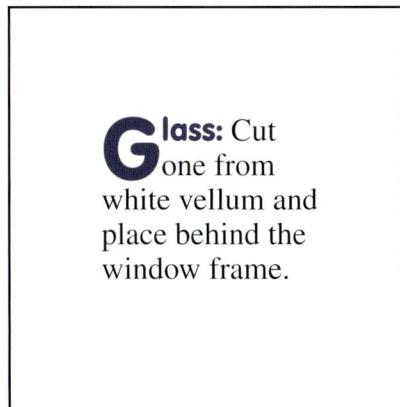

Glass: Cut one from white vellum and place behind the window frame.

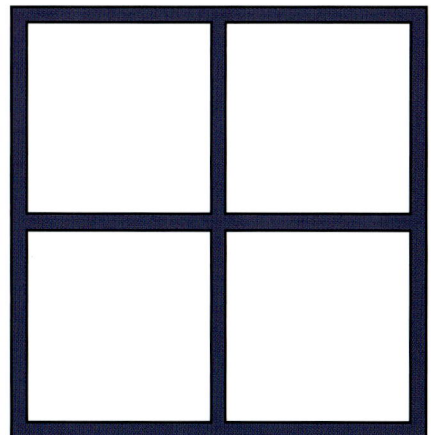

Window frame: Cut one from navy blue paper.

dripping off my chin

X | is for eXtra cute kids,

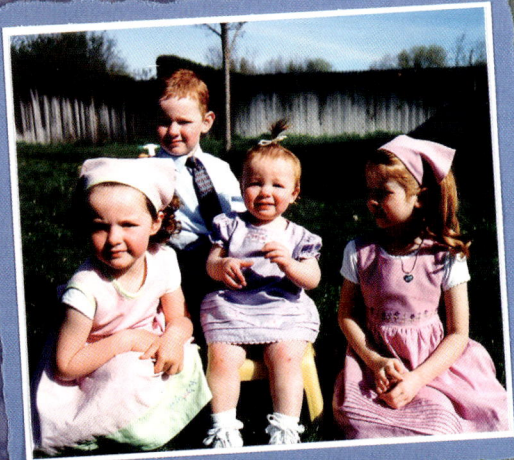

anxious for Easter to begin

You will need:

patterned Paper Pizazz®: blue stars on blue (Jacie's Watercolor Naturals, also available by the sheet)

solid Paper Pizazz®:
- medium blue, olive green (Teresa's Handpicked Solid Muted Colors)
- white (New Plain Pastels)

green decorating chalk

basic supplies (see page 1)

1 Cut a 5½"x8½" sage green rectangle. Cut a 5½"x8½" piece of stars paper and tear a left hand border (see page 1). Glue the stars paper to the olive green with the tear on the right as shown.

2 Mat your photo on white. Mat it again on blue with a torn border. Glue it centered on the page.

3 Cut out an "X" alphabet tile and chalk the checkerboard with green. Mat it onto a 1¼" white square. Glue it to the page as shown. Hand write or computer print your words on white paper. Use the black pen to add a penwork border then chalk the "X" green. Glue them to the page.

is for Yawn,

You will need:

patterned Paper Pizazz®: yellow gingham (Soft Tints, also available by the sheet)

solid Paper Pizazz®:
- navy blue (Teresa's Handpicked Solid Jewel Tints)
- sage green (Teresa's Handpicked Solid Muted Colors)
- white (New Plain Pastels)

green decorating chalk

basic supplies (see page 1)

1 Cut a 5½"x8½" navy blue rectangle. Cut a 5½"x8½" piece of gingham paper and tear a right hand border (see page 1). Glue the gingham paper to the navy with the tear on the left as shown.

2 Mat your photo on white. Mat it again on sage with a torn border. Glue it centered on the page.

3 Cut out a "Y" alphabet tile and chalk the checkerboard with green. Mat it onto a 1¼" white square. Glue it to the page as shown. Write or print your words on white paper. Use the black pen to add a penwork border then chalk the "Y" word green. Glue them to the page.

Y | is for Yawn,

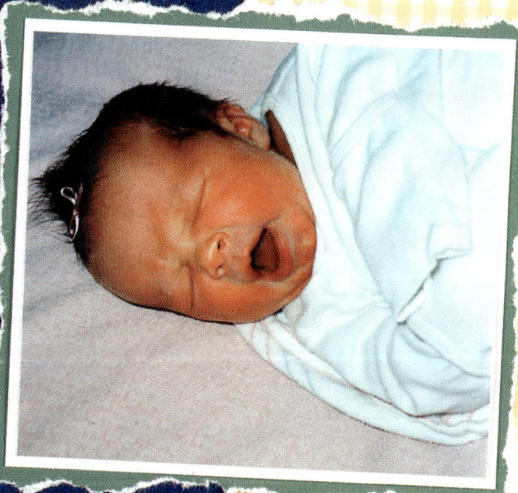

from a sleepy baby